T for Tinkercad
C for Circuit Design
Advanced

This book covers circuit design, with more complicated starter projects that can be tested out through Tinkercad Simulation. They are written to be more human while being technically accurate and useful.

Table of Contents

Why Tinkercad?

Learning electronic circuit can be tricky if you do not have the parts and components handy. The good thing about Tinkercad is that it has most of these stuff available in "virtual form" so you can "put them together" and "simulate" the actual running, all without the need to have anything actual and physical. This is absolutely perfect for beginners who are totally new to electronics!

As of today Tinkercad is totally free. You can access its website and sign up for a free account (or use an existing Google account).

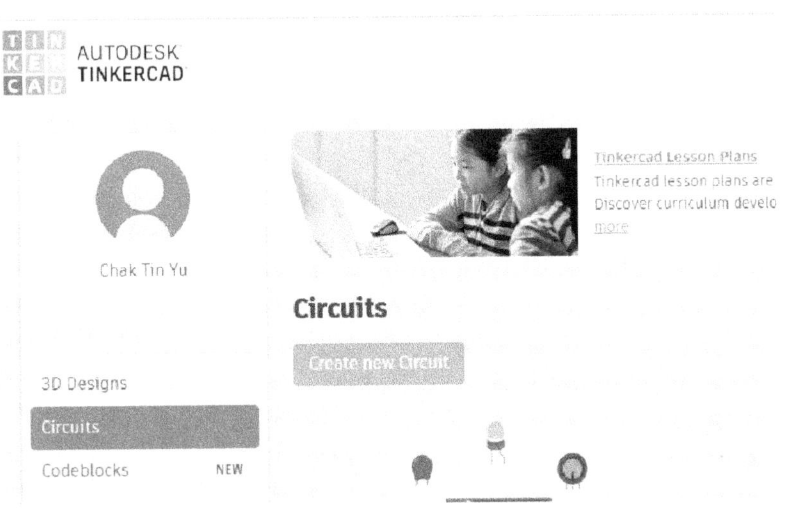

You click Create New Circuit to enter a blank workspace where starter circuits are available on the right, ready for your drag and drop operation.

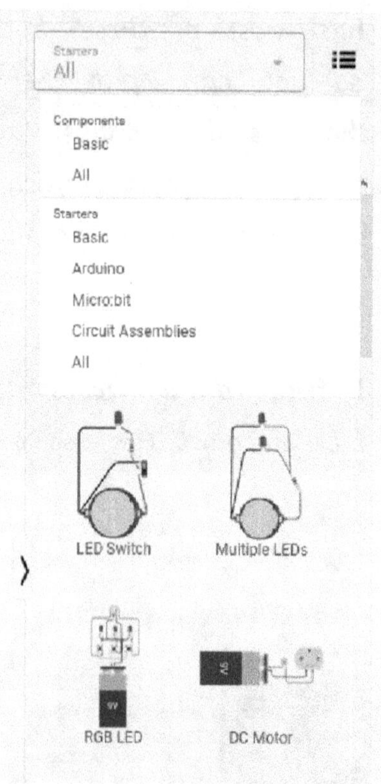

The general way to build a circuit is to drag and drop several components to the center of the work space, then click on the "contact tips" of the components to

   Copyright 2021 **Tomorrowskills.com**.

link them up. All these can be done via mouse click.

The starter circuits are prebuilt, and the easiest way to learn is to modify them bit by bit so to know the difference that can be made by adding or removing stuff.

Actual running of the circuit can be done via this button:

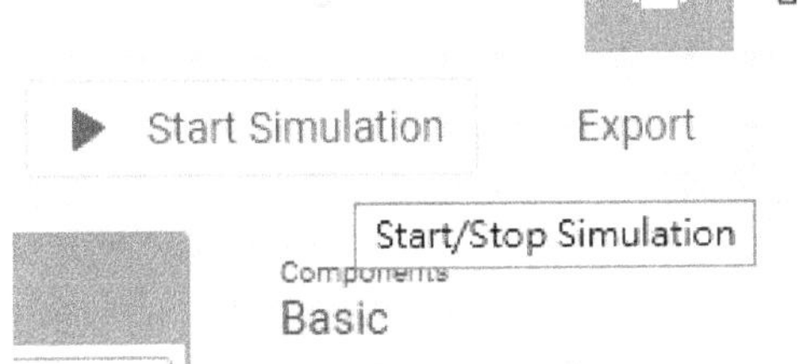

If you click Export, you can actually save a copy of your circuit to your local hard drive. The file is in BRD format.

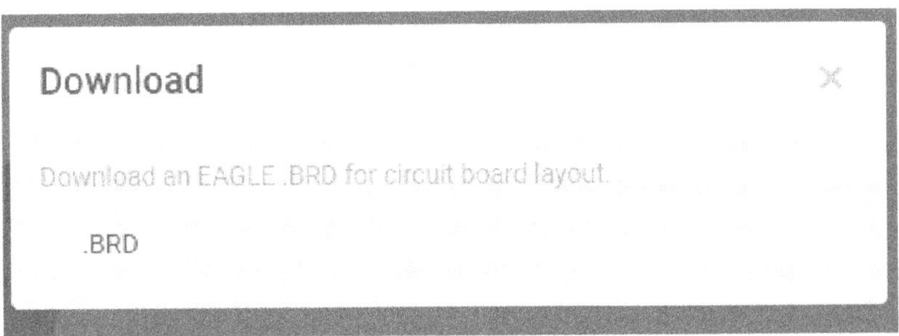

Project 1 – making a circuit adjustable (a dimmer)

This LED Light Up starter circuit is a perfect place to start. It has a resistor, a LED light and a cell.

Lets add a switch to it to enable brightness adjustment. Let's use the potentiometer component as a rotatory dial of a dimmer.

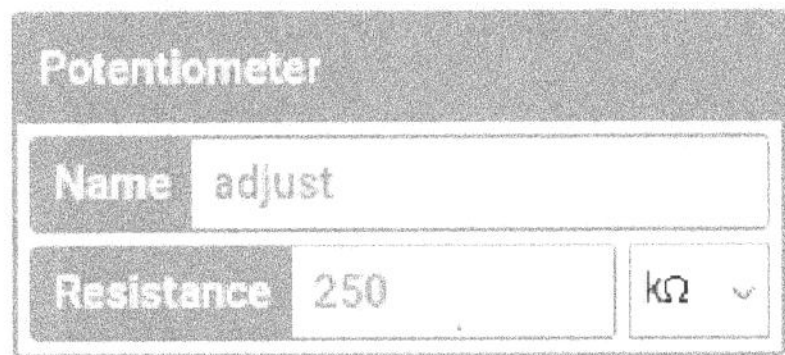

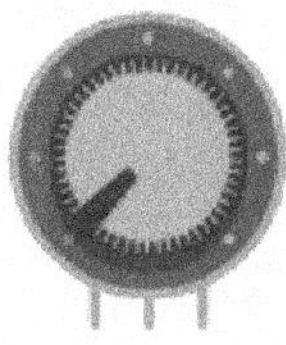

A potentiometer is basically a three-terminal variable resistor. It has a rotating contact for serving as an adjustable voltage divider. Terminal 1 is the left most contact. The middle one is called the wiper, which is part of a movable contact allowing the resistance to be changed manually (adjustment is actually done by sliding the wiper left or right). The right most one is terminal 2.

For this project you need to know that only the wiper

 Copyright 2021 **Tomorrowskills.com**.

and one of the terminals are to be used.

Refer to the configurations below, they are essentially the same, as long as the polarity to the light is correct (LED light requires correct polarity, which we have discussed in our previous book):

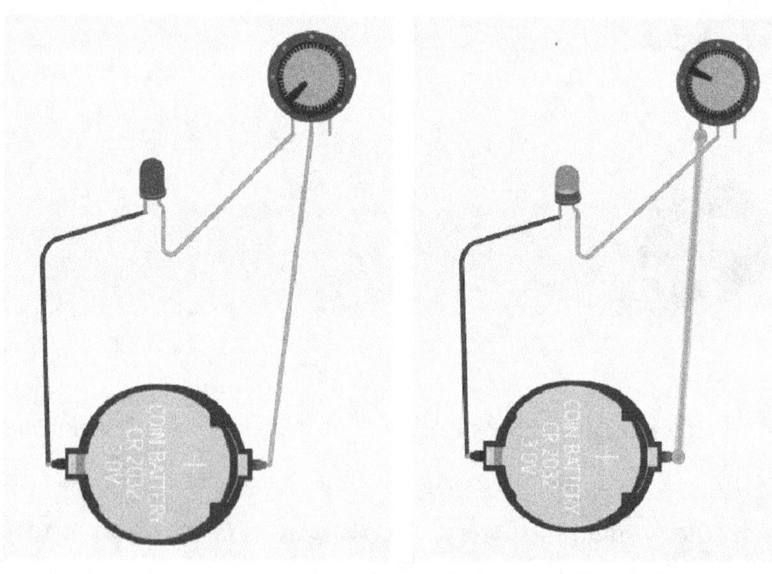

The potentiometer can be located on the POS side or NEG side of the battery connection, although normally it is placed on the POS side.

You rotate the dial and you will see the effect. Since only one terminal is involved, rotation of the dial will produce power to the light only in one direction. HOWEVER, you can actually connect the other terminal to the light as well, just like this configuration.

Another issue remains to be solved is that if we rotate the dial to the fullest there is too much power for the light (that's why you see the exclamation mark). To avoid that situation, a resistor can be added to one side of the battery connection so to weaken the power. With it, when you run the simulation you will no longer see the exclamation mark.

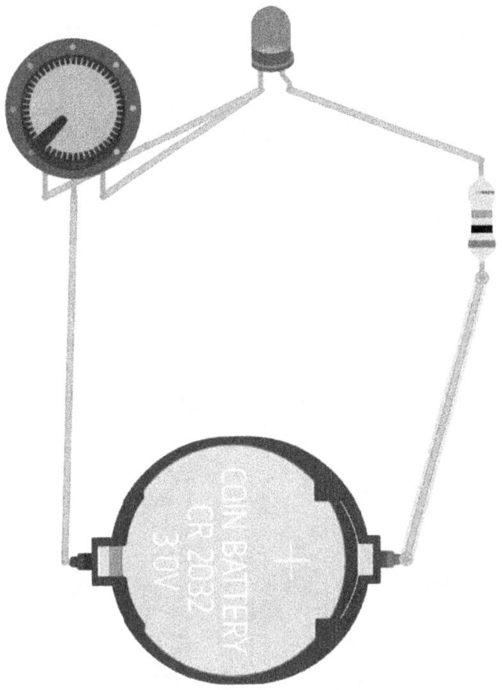

Now let's come up with a variation of this circuit so to have it support two lights. In this case the direction of rotation determines which light gets turned on.

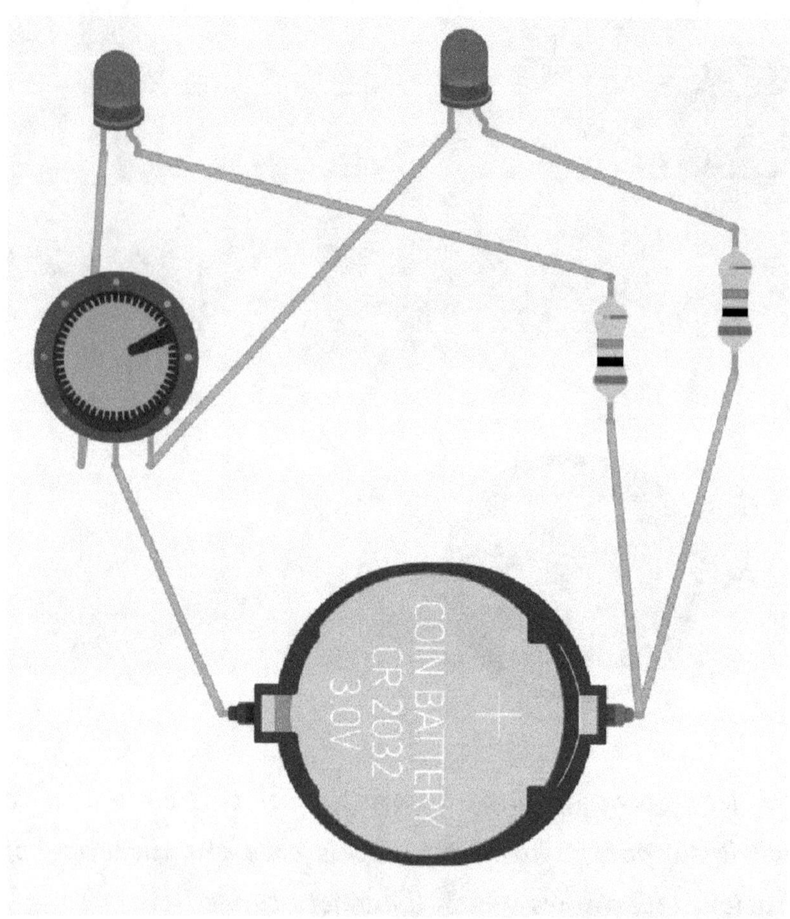

COIN BATTERY
CR 2032
3.0V

Project 2 – adding a light sensing device

This time we are forming a circuit with a photoresistor. A photoresistor is a light-dependent resistor that will decrease resistance when receiving light on its light sensitive surface. Sort of like a light sensor.

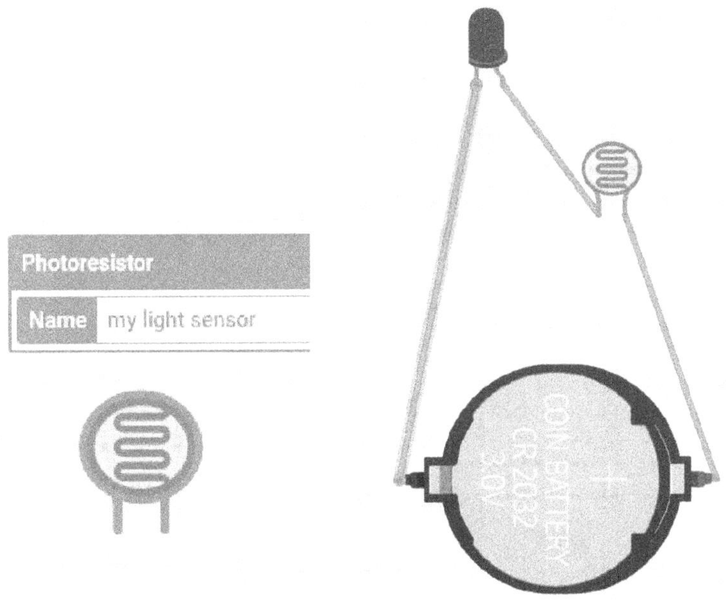

When you start simulation and click on the photoresistor, you can control the amount of light it is exposed to.

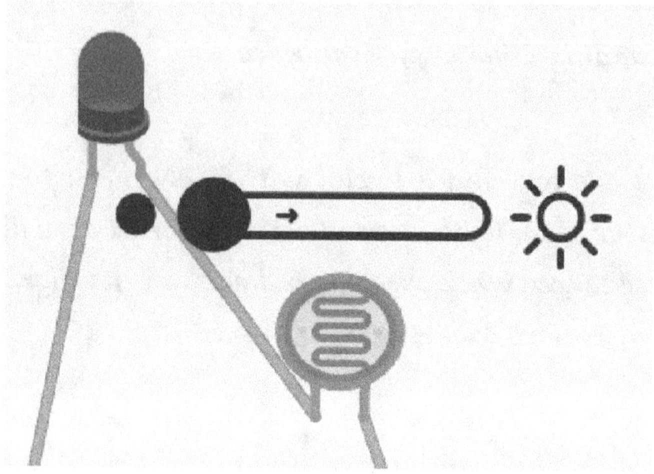

You slide the "switch" to control the "sunlight". The stronger the sunlight, the less resistance it brings to the circuit so more power goes to the LED light.

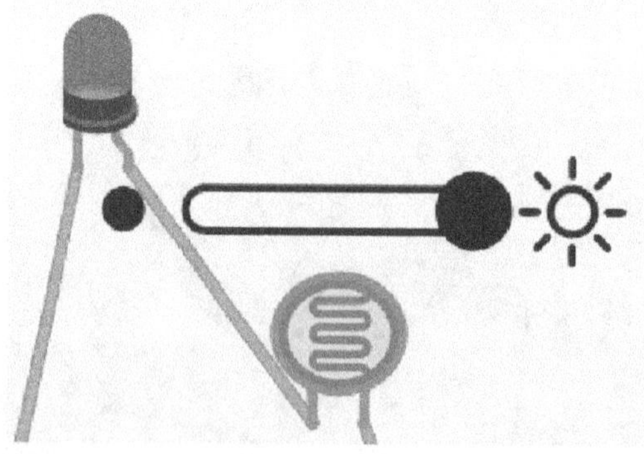

An ambient light sensor can provide similar effect here. In the real world, it is sort of a photodetector that senses the amount of ambient light ("natural" ambient sunlight and "artificial" ambient light such as street light are examples) present, and then appropriately dim a device screen (by allowing the necessary current to pass through) to match it.

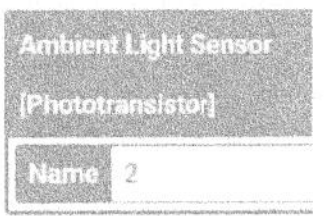

In Tinkercad, it works just like a photoresistor.

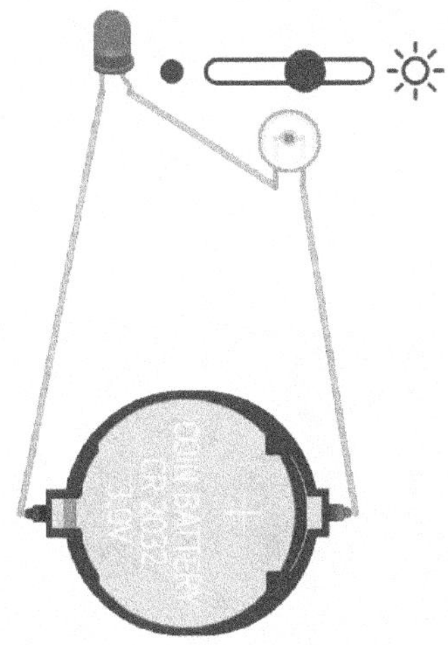

A photo diode can also serve the same purpose. HOWEVER, photo diode does care about polarity - it will not work unless the polarity is correct:

In this configuration, the battery's POS end goes to the NEG terminal of the photo diode. Then its POS terminal goes to the LED light's anode.

Project 3 - fruit batteries

Instead of using a battery, we can actually use a lemon to generate power, even though the power is weak. It is commonly used to illustrate the type of chemical reaction known as oxidation-reduction that occurs in batteries. The citric acid in the lemon can in fact act as an electrolyte.

Tinkercad provides you with a lemon battery that has very low voltage (something way below 1V) by default

   Copyright 2021 **Tomorrowskills.com**.

but you are allowed to change it (which is unrealistic).

Default:
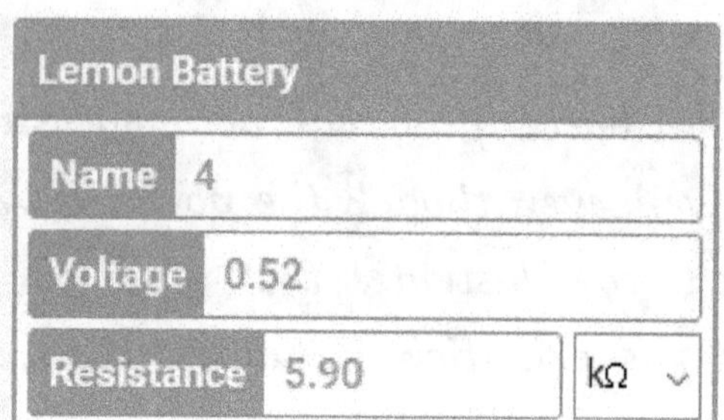

Manually changed:

A potato battery is similar - it is a source of chemical energy. Again, the default voltage is so low that unless you manually pump up the voltage it can hardly power anything!

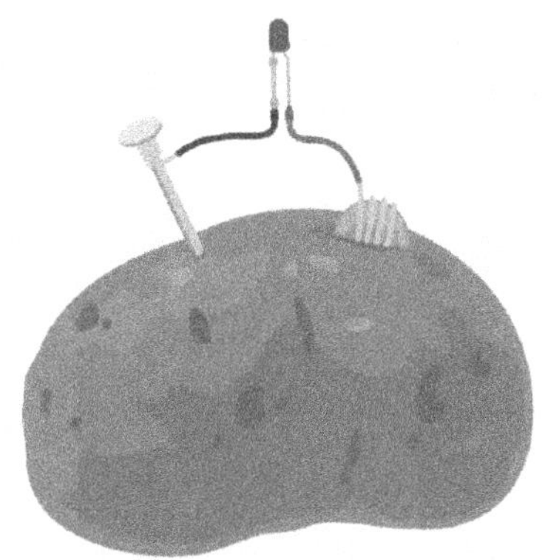

To simulate a real world condition, you can actually chain up multiple lemon/potato batteries serially so to attain a voltage that is strong enough to turn on a device:

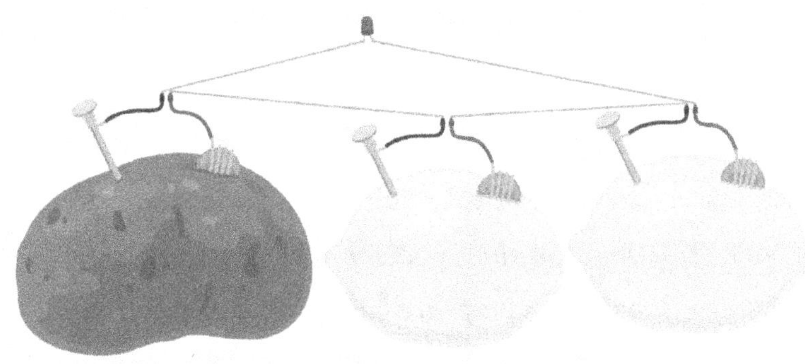

In our Tinkercad simulation, we need to have at least 3 of these connected together to power up a small LED light.

We can connect a multimeter to the configuration to find out the voltage produced:

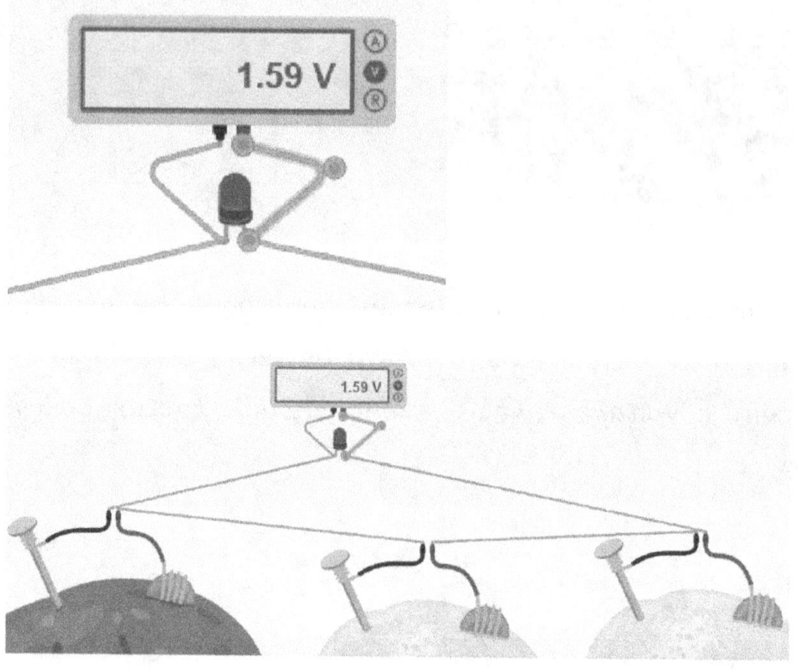

Mixing and matching potato with lemon is okay because they are simply supplying electrical power – in the context of a circuit they are almost identical "power sources" (do note that a potato can almost always produce more power than a lemon).

Project 4 - adding a polarized capacitor

In our previous starter book we talked about a simple capacitor that does not care about polarization. This time we use one that cares about it.

Since a non-polarized capacitor has no implicit polarity, it can be connected to a power source either way. A polarized capacitor has implicit polarity and it must be connected one way (or it may be damaged).

Wrong polarization:

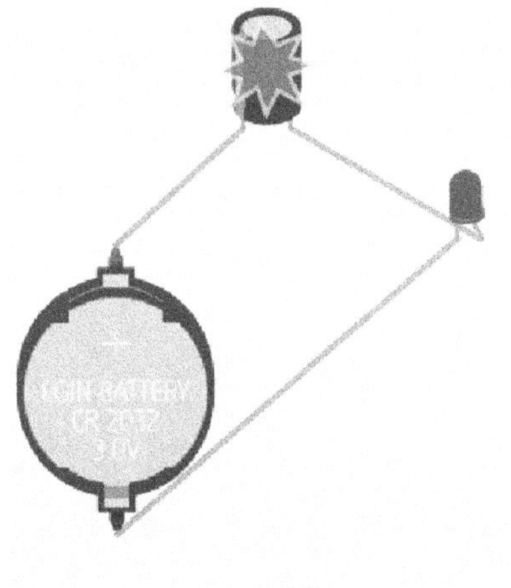

Correct polarization:

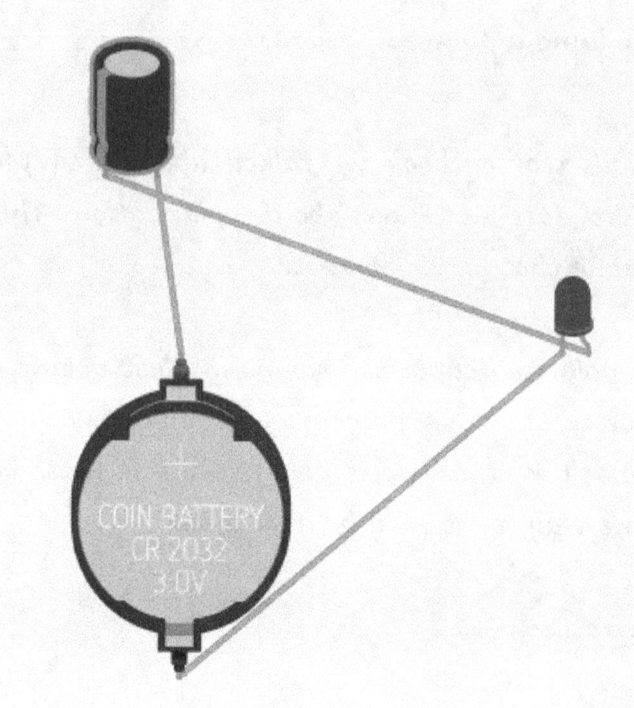

Correct polarization means the POS terminal of the capacitor is connected to the POS terminal of the battery (i.e. the power source).

A capacitor has a value of capacitance, which is the ratio of the amount of electric charge stored – a larger value usually means more current for a given voltage.

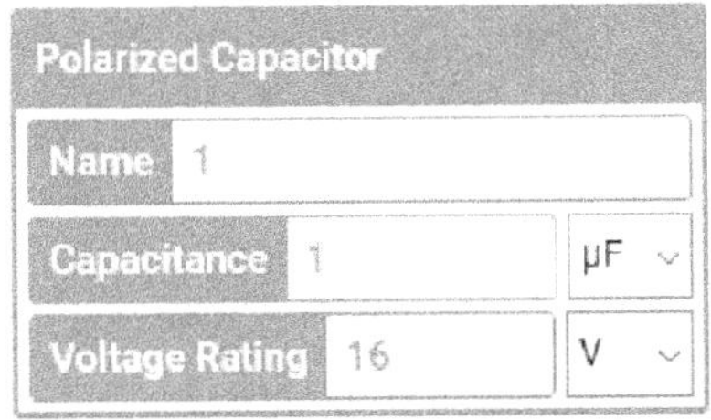

There is also a voltage rating. It does not mean it can pump up voltage. It simply means it can live with current of such voltage level.

Since incorrect polarization can damage the polarized capacitor, you want to be very careful when using it. Using a diode to protect it may not always work out. On Tinkercad, using a diode to protect a polarized capacitor doesn't seem to work as expected.

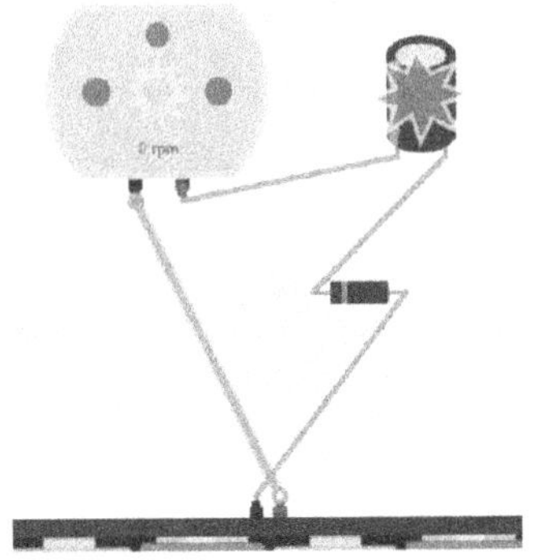

Project 5 – preventing a motor from spinning in reverse direction

There are circumstance when you want to prevent a motor from spinning towards another direction. A diode seems to be the right choice. First you need to know the direction of placement. See this symbol:

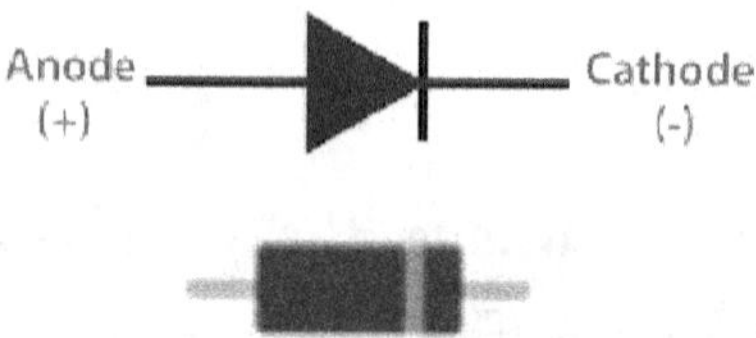

Refer to the configuration below, protection is in effect so the motor receives no power:

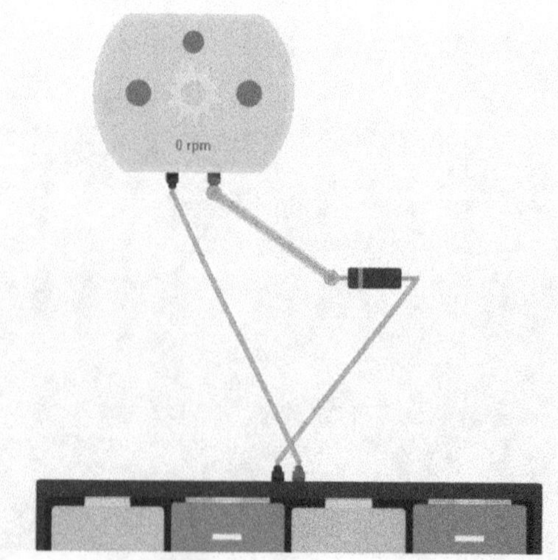

With the polarization corrected, the motor can spin now:

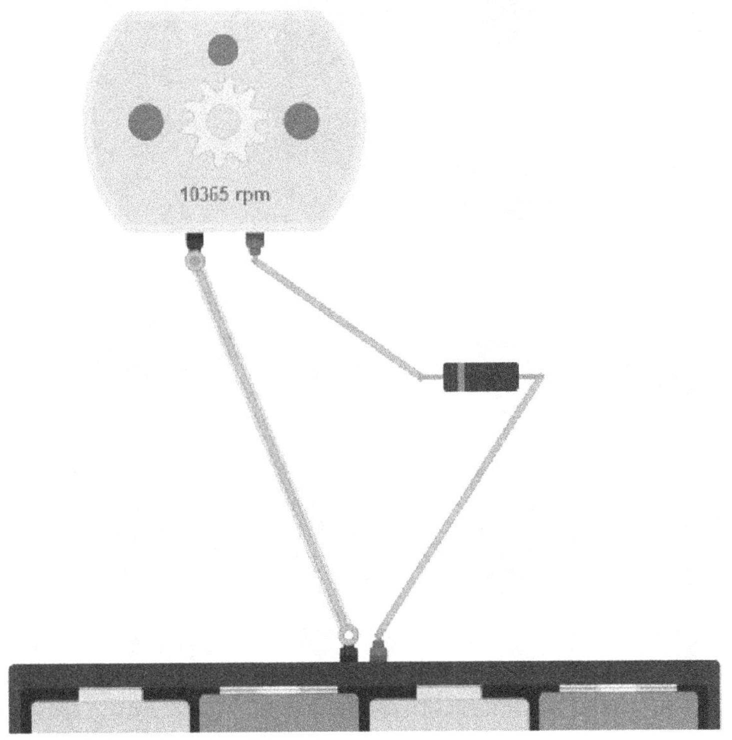

If you want to reverse the direction of rotation, you can swap the POS and NEG connections on the motor BUT NOT on the battery.

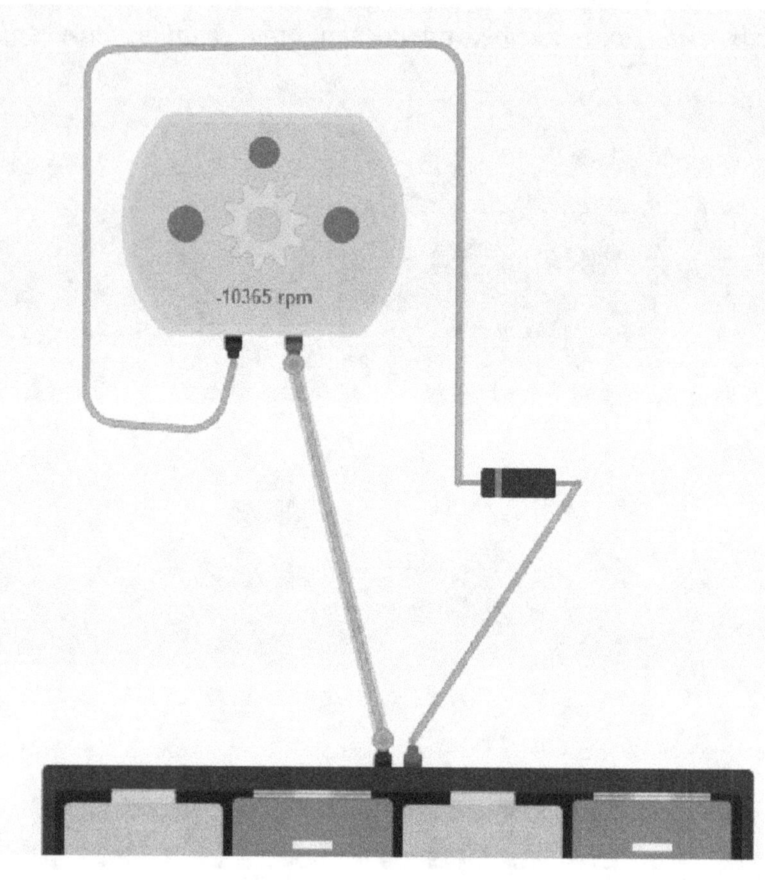

If you are installing this configuration on a model car so that each motor drives one wheel, you must make sure they spin in different directions.

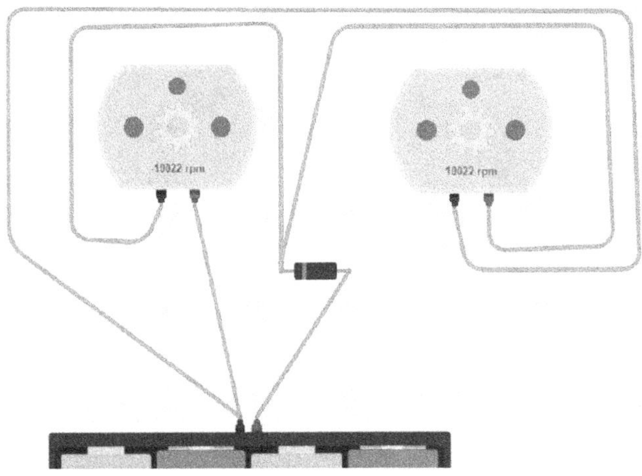

This configuration will also work:

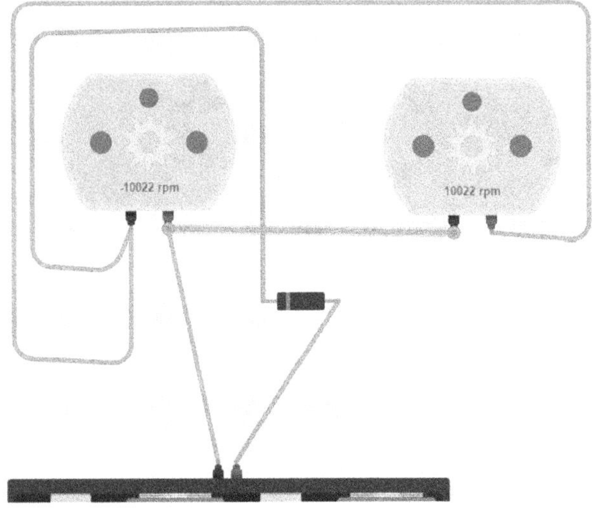

Or, an easier alternative is to use a gearmotor, which has a shaft on both sides for driving two wheels:

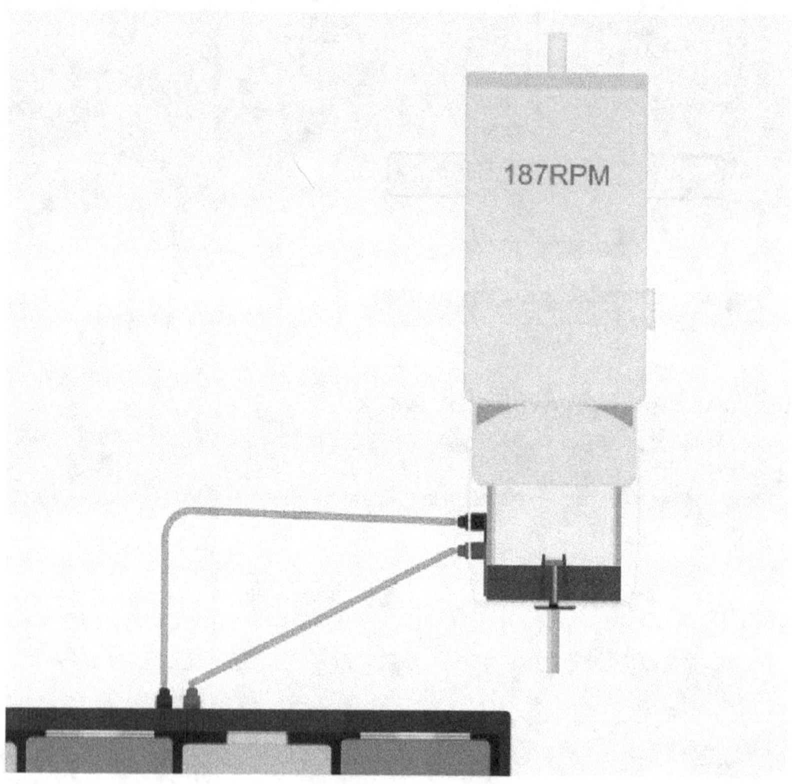

Project 6 – adding a LED light that changes color

There is a special RGB LED light with 4 terminals:

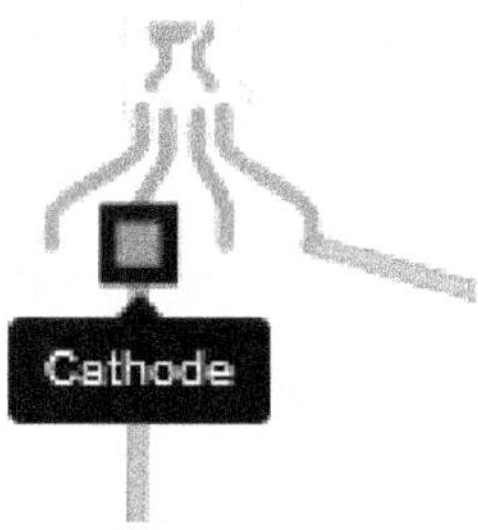

The second terminal is the cathode, which is always connected to the NEG of the battery. The other terminals are for Red, Green and Blue. A resistor must be used or you can fry it.

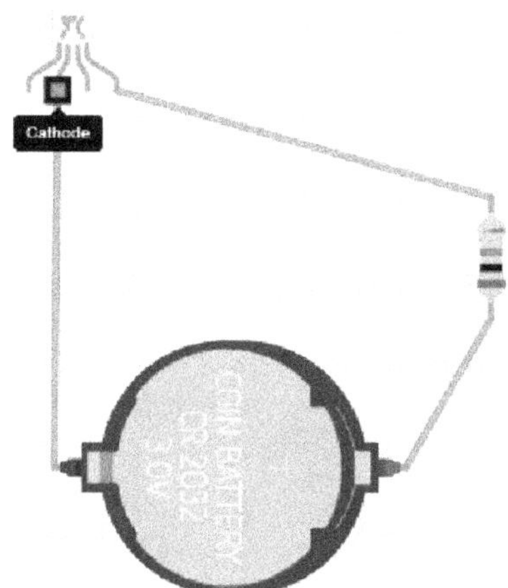

Red:

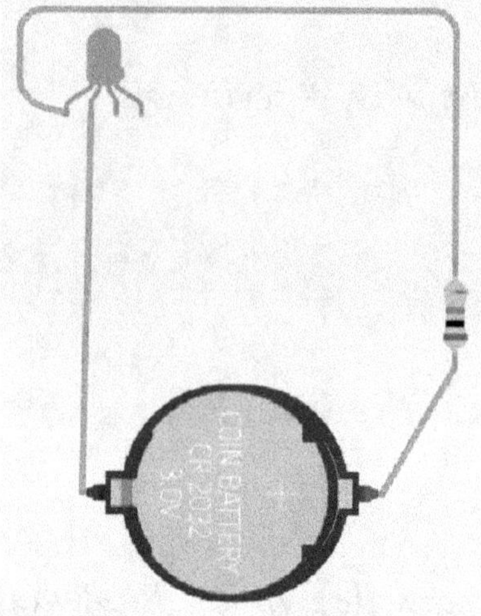

Green:

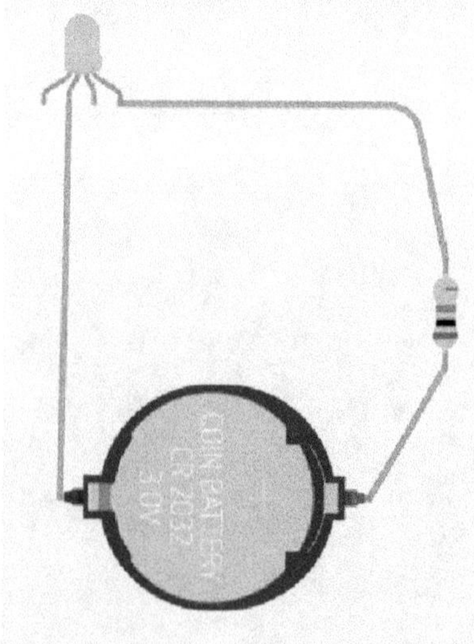

   Copyright 2021 **Tomorrowskills.com**.

Blue:

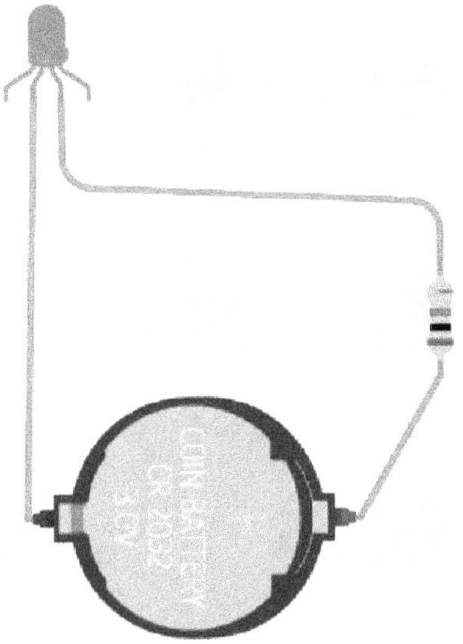

All connected:

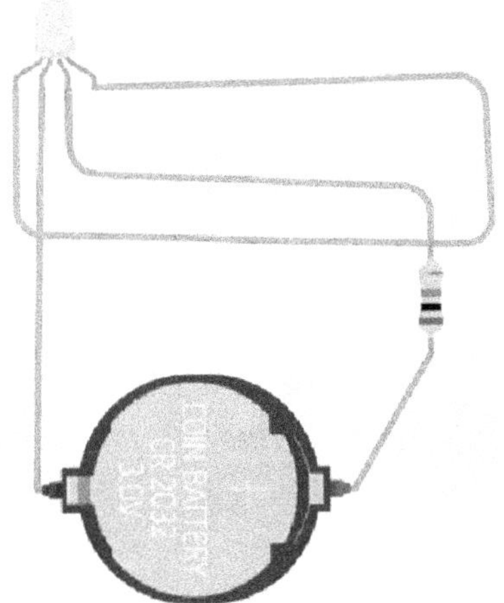

To be able to selectively switch between colors, a DIP switch can be used. It allows up to 4 pairs of connections. For a RGB light we only need to use 3 (any 3 will do).

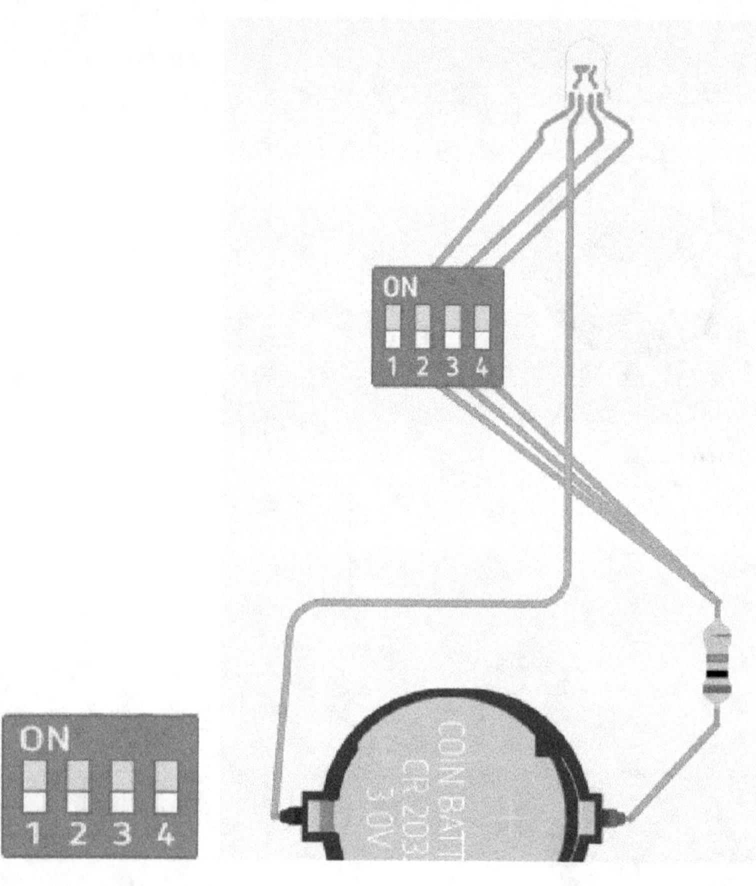

We can even use multiple LEDs with different wirings to create different color combinations! See this:

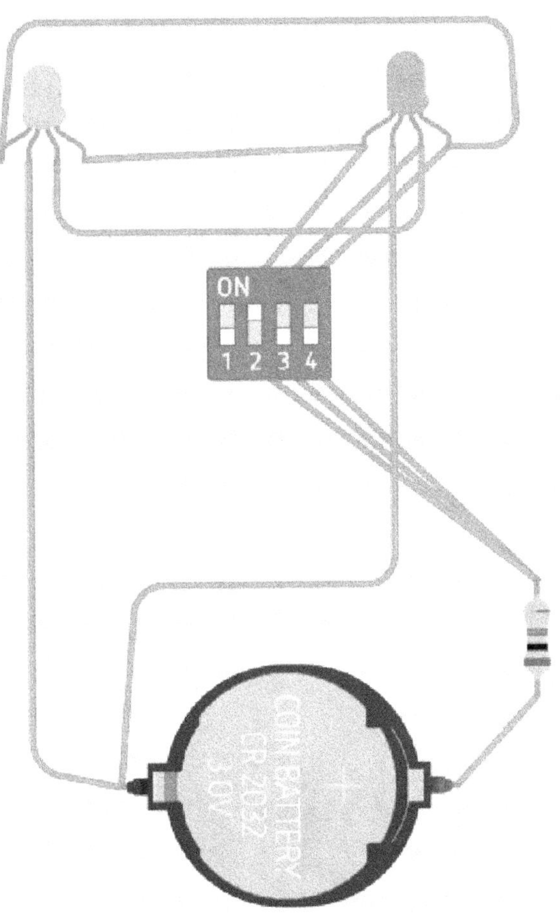

OR, you can use light sensors to activate certain color, which may be useful as some sort of room entry indicator. For example, with a light sensor placed in a room, whoever enters the room in the dark and switches on the light will trigger the sensor. You can have different colors for representing different rooms.

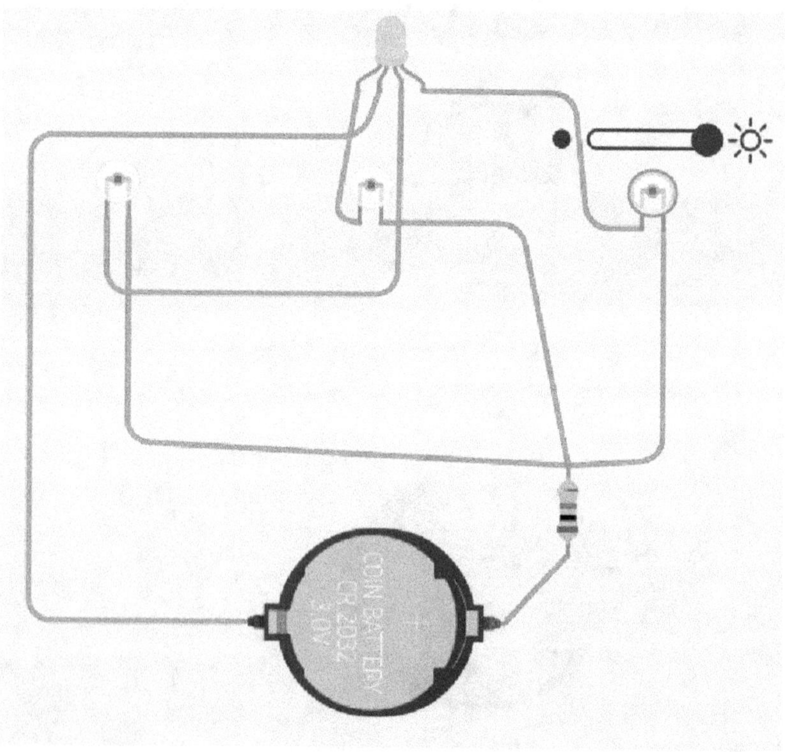

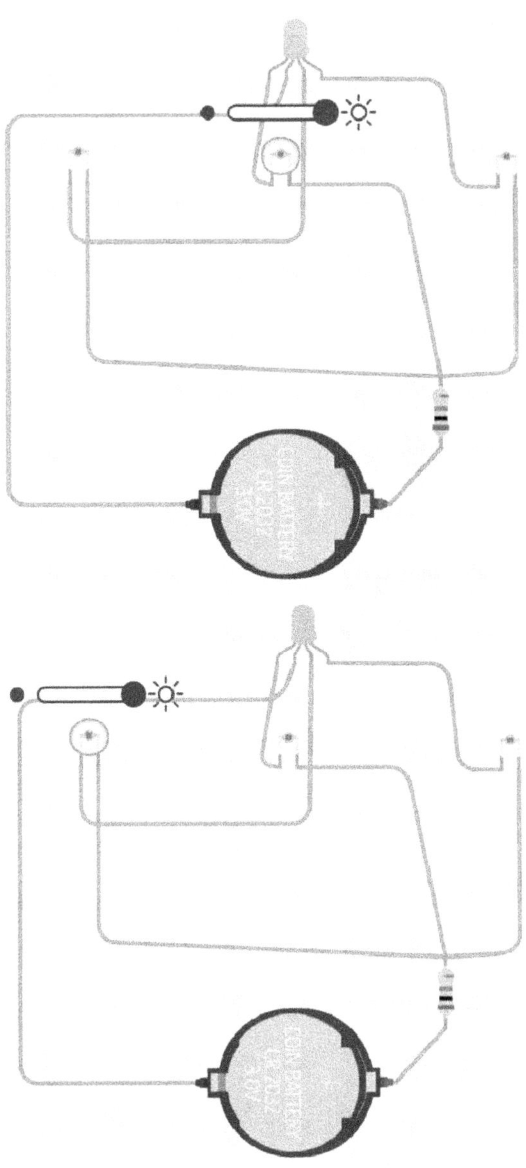

SUN BATTERY
CR 2032
3V
COIN BATTERY
CR 2032
3.0V

Project 7 – adding a temperature sensor

Tinkercad has a temperature sensor that can work under low voltage and provide a voltage output that is linearly proportional to the temperature detected.

There are 3 terminals. The left most one takes input power from the battery's POS connection. The middle one produces power output. The right most one is a GND connection, which should be connected to the battery's NEG connection. This is modelled after the real world temperature sensor known as TMP36.

The higher the temperature detected, the higher the voltage it can produce as output.

   Copyright 2021 **Tomorrowskills.com.**

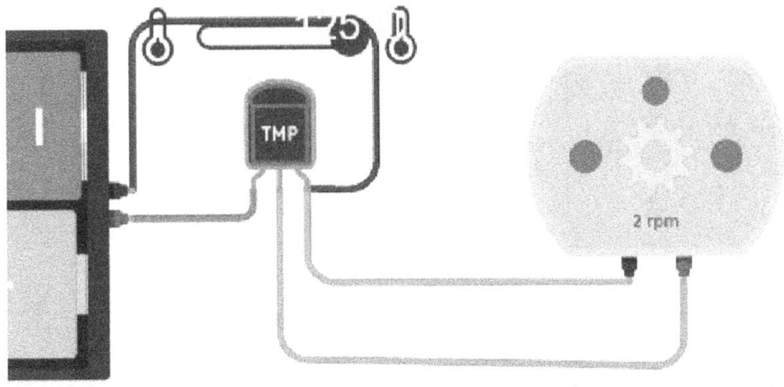

It may be useful as a detector for detecting an overheated condition. A red LED can be attached to the circuit for such an alarm system.

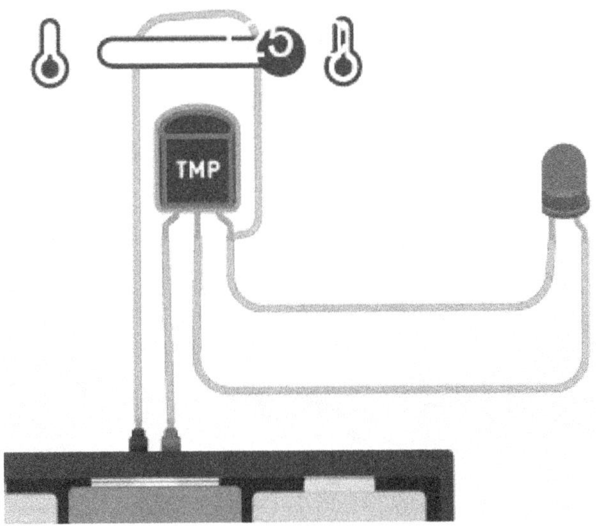

   Copyright 2021 **Tomorrowskills.com**.

Do note that this TMP36 sensor has an input limit of 5.5V. Anything over this voltage can fry the sensor. Therefore, either use max 3 x 1.5V battery, or add a resistor to it.

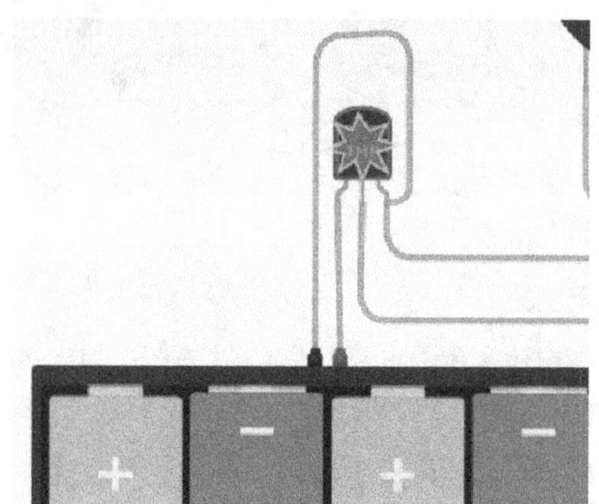

4x 1.5v:

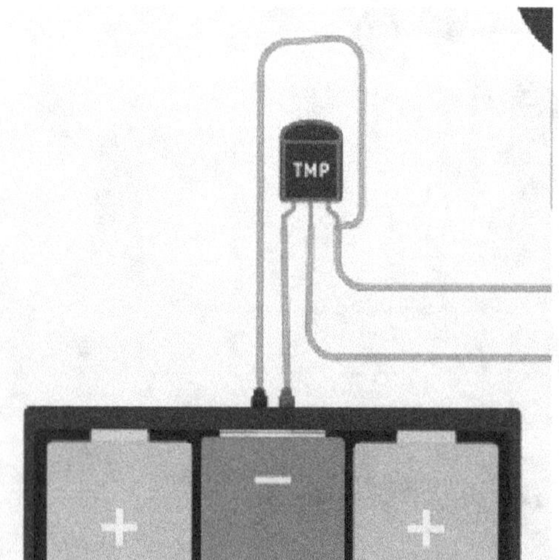

3x 1.5V:

   Copyright 2021 **Tomorrowskills.com**.

Project 8 - adding a tilt sensor

A tilt sensor can be used for measuring the change in tilt - simply put it detects orientation or inclination. You may use it to build a circuit that detects proper levelling. See this:

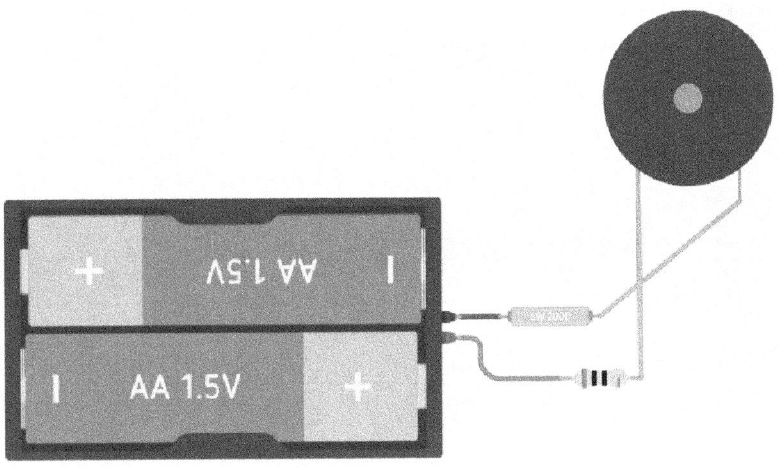

The amount of current that can pass through depends on the angle of tilt.

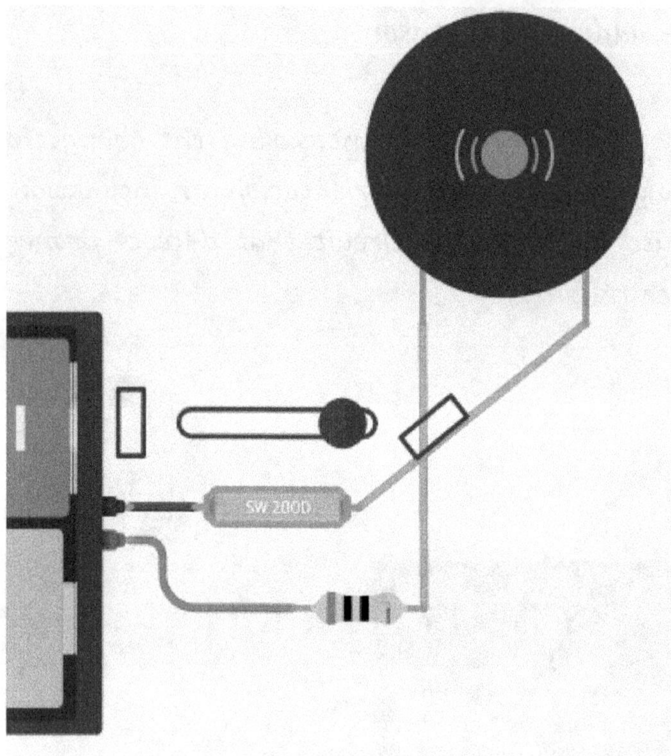

The Tinkercad version is based on the real world sensor SW-200D, which will be triggered when the tilt angle is more than 10 degree.

Project 9 - using a bread board

A breadboard allows you to design and test circuit with plug and play rather than soldering. Tinkercad has a mini breadboard that can be used for simple design.

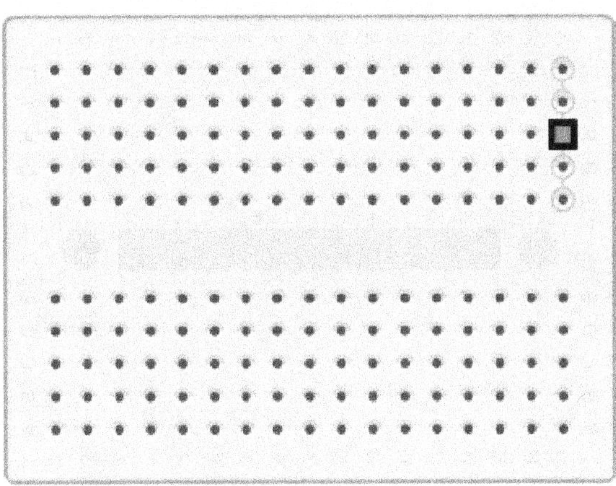

As can be seen from the photo, everything that gets plugged into the same row are interconnected by default.

   Copyright 2021 **Tomorrowskills.com**.

Therefore, the most important rule is that the battery POS and NEG connections must never sit on the same row!

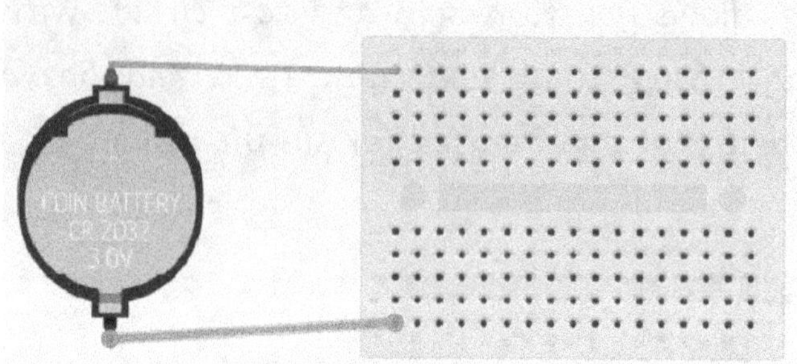

Refer to the example below, we are trying to convert a circuit into one that sits on a breadboard.

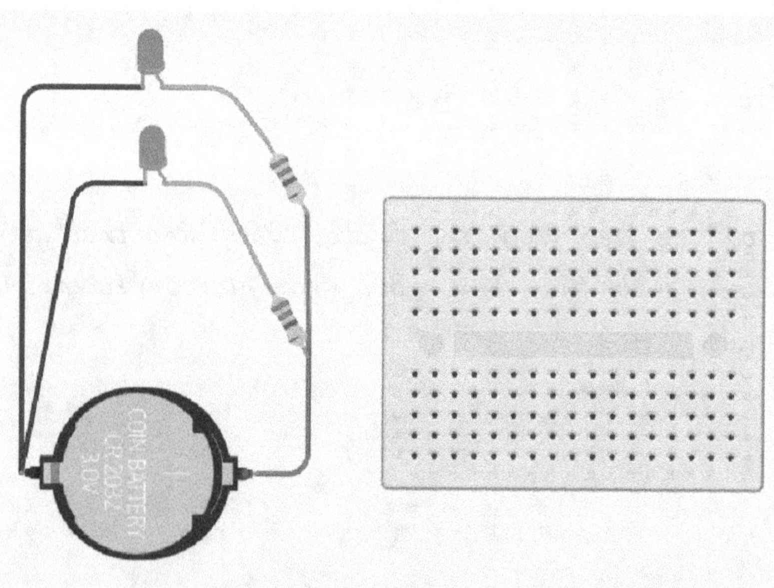

   Copyright 2021 **Tomorrowskills.com.**

This is what is done:

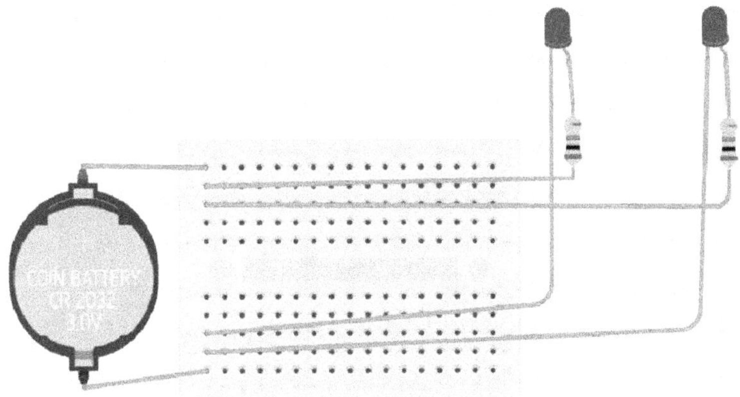

The breadboard simply provides you with a place to neatly organize the wires and the connections.

Here are some variations that can achieve the same result:

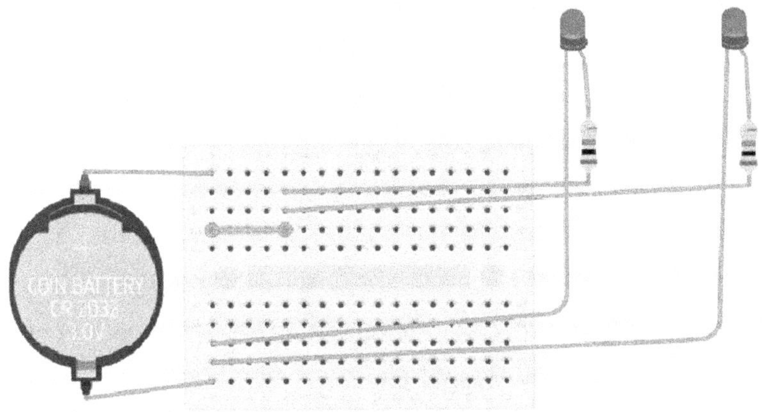

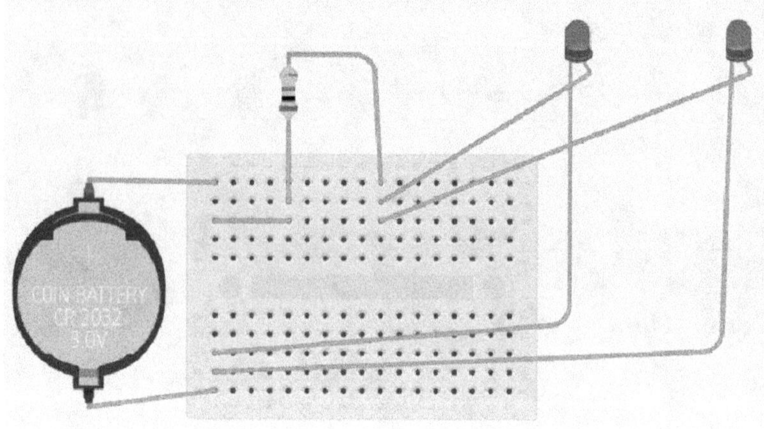

The following illustration shows what the actual connections look like:

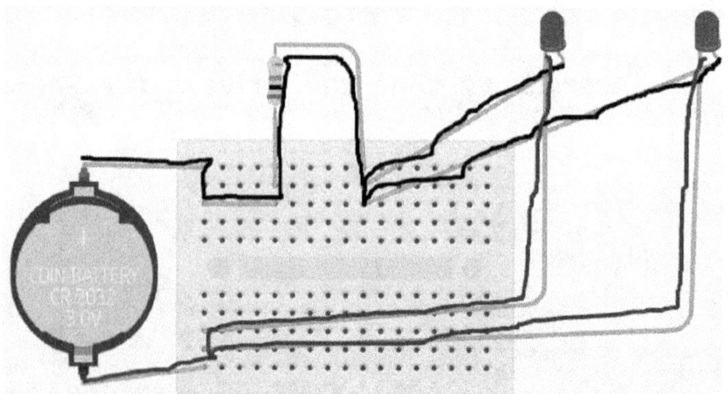

The ability to neatly layout the connections allow you to come up with more complicated circuit designs without messing up wires here and there.

Here is another example involving a sensor and a DC motor.

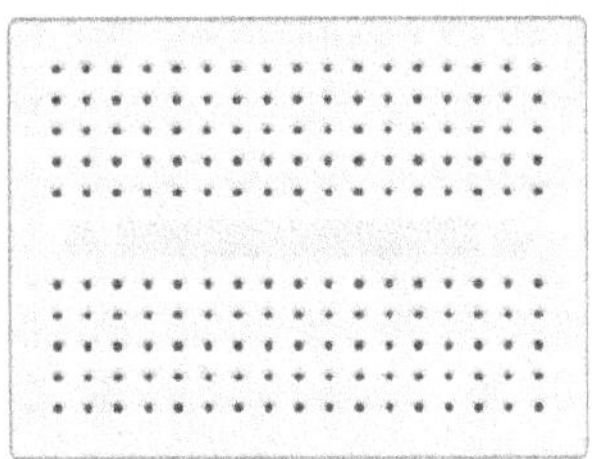

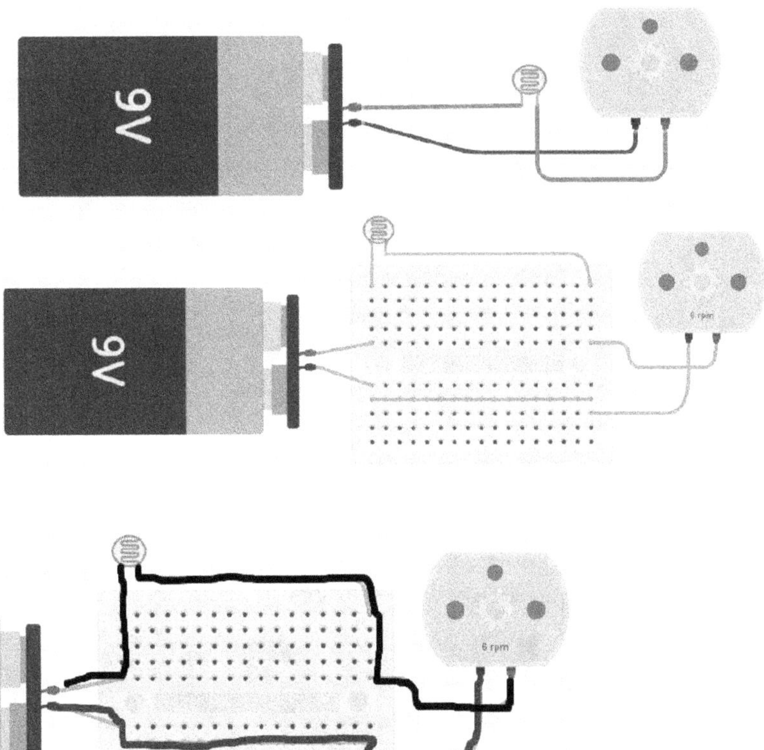

This configuration involves two batteries linked together.

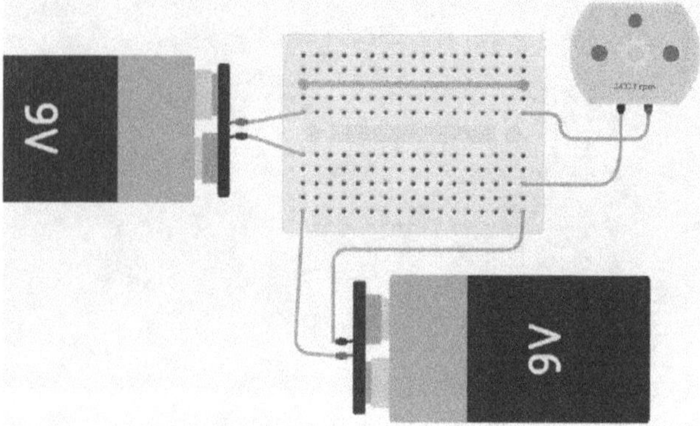

This is in fact a serial configuration where two batteries are serially connected so we effectively have something close to 9V x 2 = 18V.

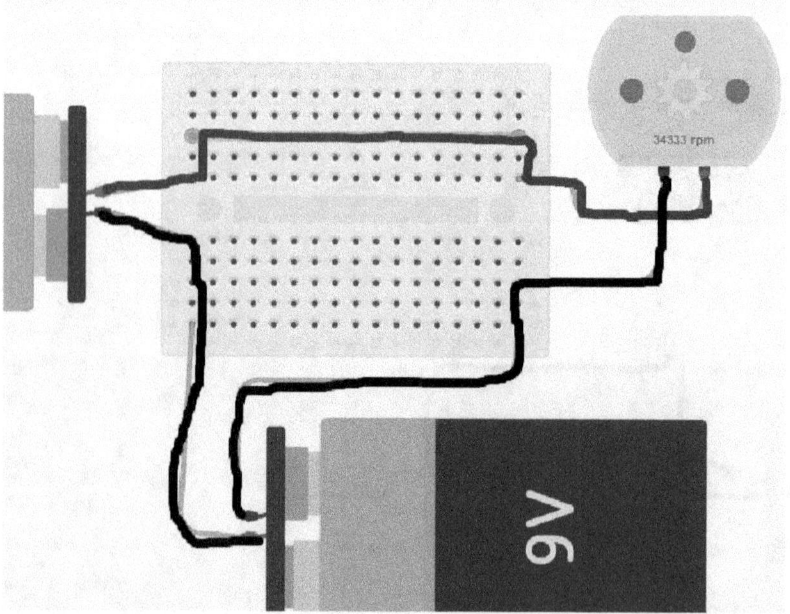

To verify, a multimeter can be added to it.

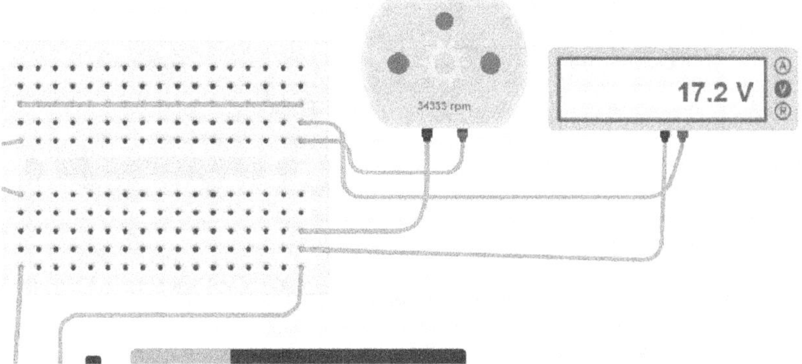

A small modification to the breadboard will change the configuration to a parallel one that produces stronger amperage without changing the voltage.

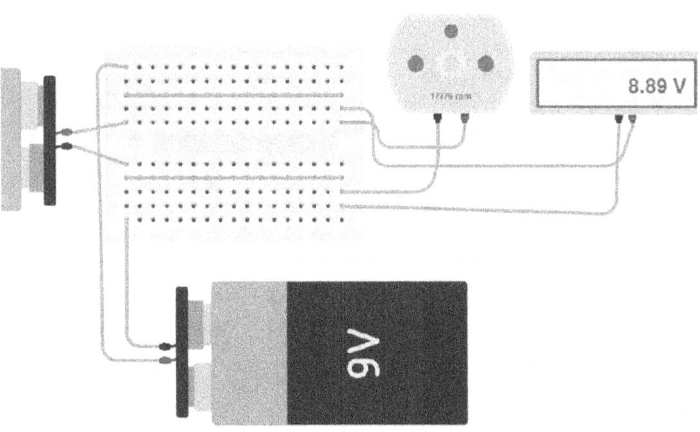

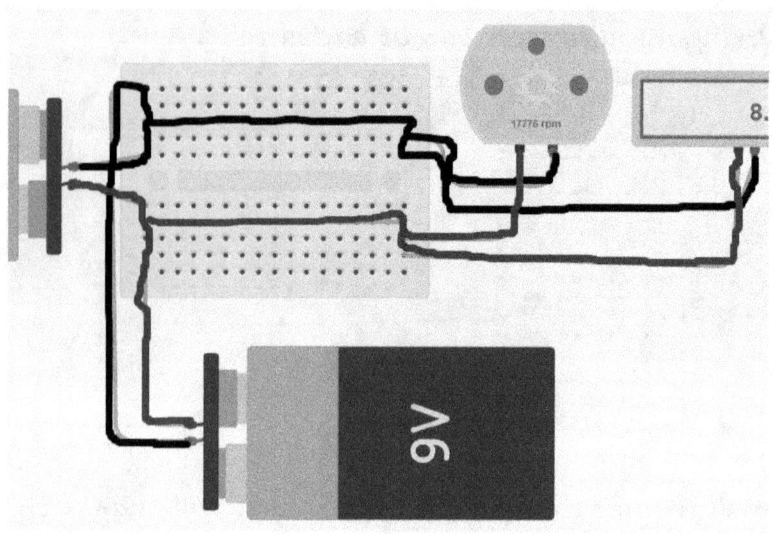

Tinkercad has several variations of the breadboard based on size. For starters, the mini one is usually good enough.

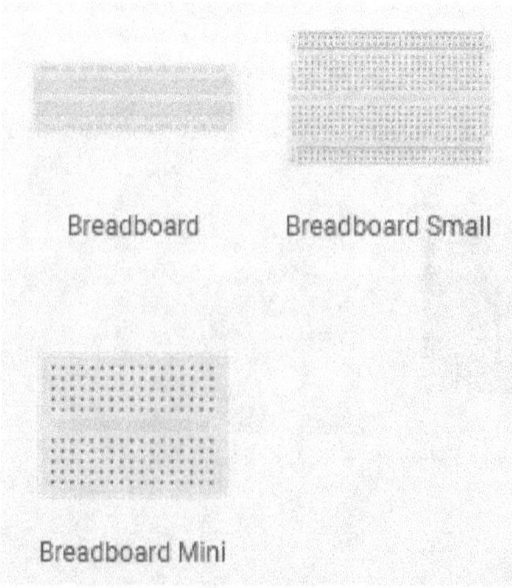

  Copyright 2021 **Tomorrowskills.com.**

END OF BOOK

Please email your questions and comments to admin@Tomorrowskills.com.